women as Healers

A history of women and medicine

Hilary Bourdillon

Humanities Inspector
for Warwickshire

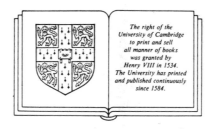

The right of the
University of Cambridge
to print and sell
all manner of books
was granted by
Henry VIII in 1534.
The University has printed
and published continuously
since 1584.

Cambridge University Press

Cambridge

New York   Port Chester   Melbourne   Sydney

Published by the Press Syndicate of the University of Cambridge
The Pitt Building, Trumpington Street, Cambridge CB2 1RP
40 West 20th Street, New York, NY 10011, USA
10 Stamford Road, Oakleigh, Melbourne 3166, Australia

© Cambridge University Press 1988

First published 1988
Reprinted 1989

Printed in Great Britain at the University Press, Cambridge

British Library cataloguing in publication data
Bourdillon, Hilary
 Women as healers : a history of women
 and medicine. – (Women in history).
 1 Medical services. Role to 1987 of
 women. Sociological perspectives
 I. Title II. Series 305.4′361

Library of Congress cataloguing in publication data
Bourdillon, Hilary.
 Women as healers.
 1. Women in medicine – History. I. Title.
R692.B676 1988 610′.88042 88-6146

ISBN 0 521 31090 3

VN

To the National Health Service

Acknowledgements

The author would like to thank the series editors Carol Adams, Paula Bartley and Cathy Loxton for their suggestions and commitment; Stephanie Boyd, CUP editor, for her support, organisation and enthusiasm; and in particular Paula Bartley and Alan Ereira for their vision and inspiration.

The author and publisher would like to thank the following for permission to reproduce copyright material: p. 4 (*Ms Reg.* 15. DI) British Library; pp.6 and 7 Ronald Sheridan's Photo Library; pp.8 and 9 (*below*) Wellcome Institute Library, London; p.9 (*above*) Fitzwilliam Museum, Cambridge; p.10 (*Ms Douce 260* Sig. Siii verso) Bodleian Library, Oxford; p.11 (*above; Ms Vienna* Codex 93. 65v) Wellcome Institute Library; p.11 (*below Ms Laud* Misc. 724. f.97), 13 (*Ms Laud* Misc. 724. f.verso) Bodleian Library; p.12 Jean Bondol Histoire ancienne, jusqu'à Cesar vol. 2 f.199 (detail), French, c.1375; p.14 (*Ms Lat.* 8846. f.106) Bibliotheque Nationale Paris; p.15 (*Ms Canon*, Misc. 476. f.27v) Bodleian Library; p.16 (*Ms Douce* p.142 Titlepage and frontispiece) Bodleian Library; p.17 Wellcome Institute Library, London; p.18 Audio-Visual Productions; p.19 His Grace The Archbishop of Canterbury and the Trustees of Lambeth Palace Library; p.21 The Mansell Collection; p.23 Museum of London; pp.24, 25, 26 Wellcome Institute Library; p.27 National Portrait Gallery, London; pp.28 and 29 Wellcome Institute Library; London; p.30 Mary Evans Picture Library; p.32 Ironbridge Gorge Museum Trust; p.34 and 36 Wellcome Institute Library, London; p.37 The Cambridgeshire Collection: Cambridgeshire Libraries; p.38 National Portrait Gallery, London; pp.40, 41, 42 Imperial War Museum; p.44 Medical Aid to Palestine

Every effort has been made to reach copyright holders; the publishers would be pleased to hear from anyone whose rights they have unwittingly infringed.

Cover illustration women surgeons and nurses at an operation during the First World War, July 1916.

Author's note

This book looks at the important role women have played in medicine in the West. Access to historical evidence and documents has necessarily been limited to those available in British archives.

To examine the part played by women world-wide would make an interesting study, but lies beyond the scope of this book.

A note on money in this book

£1 = 20s (shillings)
1s = 12d (old pence)
The old shilling has become 5 new pence. The value of money was very different in past centuries. To work out the real value you should compare the wages people received with how much they had to pay for rent, food, clothes, etc.

Glossary

Words printed in *italic* are explained in the Glossary on page 48.

Contents

Domestic medicine played an important part in people's healthcare throughout the centuries. Women making medicines and watching over a sick man, from a 14th-century manuscript, Historia Scholastica.

Introduction

When writing a history of medicine, historians generally begin with the writings of Hippocrates, who lived in Ancient Greece about 430–330 BC. His ideas influenced medicine and people's theories about diseases and cures until the 17th century.

The writings of Hippocrates, and other *physicians* who developed his theories, tell us something about the history of medical ideas. But they do not necessarily tell us about the ways in which people treated disease, or about the medical treatment which was available to the majority of people.

The people who studied the writings of Hippocrates and his followers, based their medical knowledge on the theory that disease was caused by an imbalance in the four humours (or moods) which controlled the body: *sanguine, choleric, melancholic* and *phlegmatic*. These four humours were associated with four liquids in the body: blood, yellow bile, black bile and phlegm.

Hippocrates' theory said that a patient could be made healthy by balancing these humours. If the physician thought that the patient's illness was caused by too much blood, for example, he would remove it by *bleeding*.

Generally the people who studied this theoretical medicine studied at university, although as printing made books more widely available in the 15th century, it was possible for those rich enough to afford a library to study medical texts at home. Very few of these people were women. Women were not in general allowed to study at university until the 19th century, although a few did study at universities in Italy before that time.

Hippocrates' influence on medical ideas was widespread, but very few people could afford to pay for treatment from a physician who had studied at university. Most people relied on being healed in the home. The women of the household had a particular responsibility for healing. Most communities also had a 'wise-woman' to whom people turned for help. The wise-woman's knowledge of medicine and cures did not necessarily come from books. She learned her work from watching and helping other healers. Wise-women found out from experience which cures worked and which did not. These healers mainly used herbal medicines rather than methods like bleeding to treat their patients.

The evidence

Domestic medicine and the healing by wise-women played an important part in people's healthcare throughout the centuries. It may seem surprising that more has not been written about it, or about the women who carried out the healing.

Can you think of any reasons why written accounts of the history of medicine might ignore women's contributions? How significant do you think the following factors are?

- Historians have generally been men, and so have tended to write about the public world in which men played a greater part, rather than the private domestic world.

- Historians have tended to concentrate on the impact of individuals in history, great men and great women. Ordinary lives, and the everyday activities of ordinary people – women and men – have not been given so much attention.

- The evidence which comes from legal records and the writings of physicians, indicates that they jealously guarded the privileges of the growing medical profession.

In this book you will find a lot of evidence about women's role in healing and medicine through the ages. You have to work out what that role was and how important it is in the history of medicine.

1   Healing in the Ancient World

People's earliest explanations of disease were religious. They thought that sickness and health were caused and created by the supernatural. When people were ill, they prayed to the gods and goddesses to help them get better. It is interesting to note that the deities who were worshipped for their powers of healing by the Ancient Minoans, Cretans and Greeks were often female. Ishtar the Assyrian goddess, for example, was both the goddess of health and the mother goddess. The priests and priestesses who served the deities in the temples, gave healing potions to people who were sick.

Women healers in Ancient Egypt

Some evidence of women's work as healers in Ancient Egypt comes from paintings in tombs and from objects found in graves. A painting in the tomb of Rameses III, for example, shows the goddess Isis healing, with priestesses as her helpers. Isis was a great goddess of nature, and the Egyptians also worshipped her as their healer. Prayers to Isis played an important part in the treatment of illness. Below is a recipe for a cure for headaches, made by the goddess Isis for the god Ca himself, in order to drive away the pains in his head:

Coriander berries	1
Berries from Xaset plant	1
Wormwood	1
Berries of the Sames plant	1
Juniper berries	1
Honey	1
To be mixed and smeared on the head.	

Ebers Papyrus, c.1560 BC

Potions like these probably owed any success they had to the patient's faith in being cured, rather than their value as medicine.

Throughout the Dynastic period of Ancient Egypt (c.3100–2686 BC), the healers were priestesses. The priestesses got their healing powers from the goddesses. By 1570 BC, however, women were to be found in the temples only as musicians, not as priestesses. Why should the priestess-healers have disappeared?

Between the 3rd and 2nd centuries BC, Egypt and the surrounding territories were invaded and many religious and cultural practices changed. This might explain the disappearance of the priestess-healer.

Medicine was not as closely linked with religion in the 3rd and 2nd centuries BC as it had been in the earlier Dynastic period. The development of the practice of *embalming* might have contributed to this change in medicine. The technique of embalming was perfected after 2300 BC. Embalmers were

The Egyptian goddess Thueris who protected pregnant women during pregnancy and childbirth. She is represented as a pregnant hippopotamus, standing upright, holding a symbol which signifies protection.

6

Sennufer, High Priest of Memphis (in Egypt) and Heliopolis (now in Lebanon), and his wife, from a tomb painting, 18th Dynasty (c. 1450 BC). Sennufer's wife is giving him symbols of magic and healing, including a scarab (beetle), in preparation for the after-life. In what way is this picture useful to a historian of medicine? What difficulties do you face in understanding it?

always men, and this work gave them a specialist knowledge of anatomy. They wrote all this information down and passed it on to other embalmers and *surgeons*, who were also men. Women were not involved in this work.

One area of healthcare which had always been in women's hands, and remained so, was midwifery. This aspect of healing had not necessarily been part of the priestess-healer's work. Mystery surrounded conception, but not childbirth. Also, midwifery was a skill which could be learned, so it was viewed differently from the power the priestess-healer needed to treat illnesses.

Although the midwives were not priestesses, they still used prayers and charms to help them in their work and to ward off the demons who might harm the mother and baby. One charm, said to ease pain in labour, ended with these instructions:

Say the words [the charm] four times over a dwarf of clay to be placed on the forehead of the woman who is giving birth.

Leiden Papyrus, c. 2nd century BC

Women healers in Ancient Greece

The writings and vase-paintings which have survived give us an idea of what life was like for women in Ancient Greece. Most Greek women worked in the home, where they prepared the food, spun and wove woollen

Terracotta statue of a woman giving birth to a baby, 6th century BC. She is being held by the midwife. What does this statue tell us about midwifery? Notice the position in which the woman is giving birth.

cloth, looked after their children and managed their household slaves. Poorer women worked in various trades, and some were employed as nurses and midwives.

As in Ancient Egypt, there was a close connection in early Greece between healing and religion. The most famous healing god was Asclepius. His two daughters, Hygieia and Panacea were goddesses of healing.

Women played a part in nursing and healing too. In the epic poem the **Iliad**, Homer describes how women washed the injuries of the wounded and covered them with sedative dressings. Homer also mentions a healer, Agamede:

Agamede, with the golden hair,
A leech [healer] was she, and well she knew,
All herbs on ground that grew.

*Homer, **Iliad**, XI 740, c. 6th century* BC

Statue of the Greek goddess Hygieia, who personified Health. What symbol of medicine, which is still in use today, is Hygieia holding? What word, based on her name, do we also use today?

There is evidence from other sources that women were involved in healing, as this tombstone inscription shows:

Phanostrate, a midwife and physician, lies here. She caused pain to none and all lamented her death.
Athens, 4th century BC

From the 3rd century BC, the ideas of Hippocrates and the influence of the two medical schools at Cos and Cnidus dominated Greek medicine. This tradition is well documented and it is easier for historians to learn about the medicine of the medical schools than other forms of healing. Women were not allowed into the medical schools. It is likely that their skills at healing were passed on by word of mouth.

The Roman tradition

It was the responsibility within Roman households for the **pater familias** (head of the household) to provide medical treatment for everyone in the household. Rich families would pass this responsibility on to a physician. The richer families in Rome employed doctors who came to Rome from the Greek medical schools. After the 1st century BC, the Romans began to found their own medical schools which taught along the lines of Hippocrates' teachings.

Women did not take part in this medical training, although upper-class women in Rome were well-educated. All women had the opportunity to work in a variety of trades. Again tombstone evidence indicates that some of them worked as healers:

TO MY HOLY GODDESS.
TO PRIMILLA, A PHYSICIAN,
DAUGHTER OF
LUCIUS VIBIUS MELITA.
SHE LIVED FORTY-FOUR YEARS,
OF WHICH THIRTY WERE SPENT
WITH LUCIUS COCCEIUS APTHORUS
WITHOUT A QUARREL.
APTHORUS BUILT THIS
MONUMENT FOR HIS BEST, CHASTE
WIFE AND FOR HIMSELF.

Rome, 1st/2nd century AD

FAREWELL, LADY PANTHIA, FROM YOUR HUSBAND. AFTER YOUR DEPARTURE, I KEEP MY LASTING GRIEF OF YOUR CRUEL DEATH. HERA, GODDESS OF MARRIAGE, NEVER SAW SUCH A WIFE: YOUR BEAUTY, YOUR WISDOM, YOUR CHASTITY. YOU BORE ME CHILDREN COMPLETELY LIKE MYSELF; YOU CARED FOR YOUR BRIDEGROOM AND YOUR CHILDREN; YOU GUIDED STRAIGHT THE RUDDER OF LIFE IN OUR HOME AND RAISED HIGH OUR COMMON FAME IN HEALING – THOUGH YOU WERE A WOMAN, YOU WERE NOT BEHIND ME IN SKILL. IN RECOGNITION OF THIS, YOUR BRIDEGROOM, GLYCON BUILT THIS TOMB FOR YOU.

Panthia, Pergamum, 2nd century AD

Roman amulet of a woman in childbirth (actual size). This piece of jewellery, made of blue glass, was probably worn as a charm, and was found in Egypt. Compare this picture with the one below. What do you notice about the positions the women have adopted for giving birth?

Women healers were popular amongst the Romans. The historian, Pliny the Elder, praises three: Elephantis, Salpe, and Sotira. They were not only midwives, but were also skilled at curing a wide range of diseases using traditional remedies.

After the 5th century AD when the power of the Roman Empire had collapsed, and the Goths and Huns from eastern Europe moved west to settle, the medical ideas of Hippocrates and his followers were lost. But some of the ideas were kept alive and developed by the Arabs in the Muslim Empire. They were not known again in western Europe until trade with Muslims brought Europeans into contact with Arab medicine in the 11th century.

Roman marble relief showing a mother, midwife and newly-born baby. At the end of the couch is a wash-basin on a stand.

2 Women healers in the Middle Ages

Household cures

From the peasant woman to the Lady of the Manor, women were skilled at making medicines and midwifery. Diagnosing illness and making cures was not something out of the ordinary, but part of their everyday work. The herbal remedies they used, like the *bleeding* used by the physicians, sometimes did more harm than good, and many of them were useless. However, some of the herbs and plants used in the household cures, such as witch-hazel, rosemary and thyme, are still respected for their healing qualities today.

Everyday work: a woman using a herbal preparation to get rid of head lice in a boy's scalp. Illustration from a German book, Hortus Sanitatis, *1491.*

Medicine and the Lady of the Manor

Margaret Paston ran her family's estate in Norfolk with her husband. Often he was away in London on business. Their letters, written between 1441 and 1447, provide a valuable source of information on the cures dispensed by the Lady of the Manor.

The Paston men wrote home for cures. John, Margaret Paston's son, wrote a hurried letter to his wife Margery:

I pray you in all haste possible to send me by the next sure messenger you can get, a large plaster of flose ungewentorum [a herbal poultice] for the King's Attorney, James Hobart . . . But when you send me the plaster, you must send me in writing how it should be laid to and taken from his knee, and how long the plaster will last goode and whether he must lape any more clothes about the plaster to keep it warm or not.

The Paston Letters

Herbal remedies and cures in easy-to-use ointments and plasters (thick pastes applied on the skin) are among the cures mentioned in the Paston letters. Some of the ingredients for these were sent from London. In 1451, Margaret wrote to her husband asking him for some 'Ungwentum album', a popular ointment used for scalds and burns. She also requested 'treacle' imported from Genoa. This was popular for treating the plague.

The importance of diet is mentioned in these letters. Margaret advises her husband to be, 'well dieted of mete and drynke, for this is the greatest help that you can have now for your health.'

Other advice shows that Margaret Paston was familiar with the theory common at that time, that 'bad air' was the cause of disease. She wrote to John asking for a 'booke with cherdeqweyns [a preserve made from quinces],' for her to use in the morning, because, 'the airs be not wholesome in this towne'.

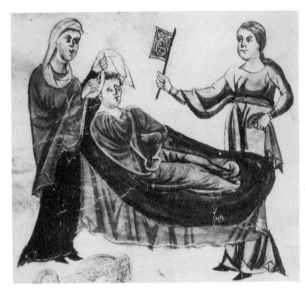

Women treating a sick man. One is applying a cold compress and the other is fanning him. Illustration from a Viennese 14th-century manuscript.

Midwives

The care of women in childbirth was part of women's work throughout the Middle Ages. Not all midwives were as famous as 'Margery Cobbe, obstetrix. Devon'. She is mentioned in the Royal Household Accounts around 1470. She attended Elizabeth, the wife of King Edward IV, and was so highly thought of that she was granted an annual pension of £10. The lives of most midwives, like other ordinary working women and men, have gone unrecorded.

A midwife learnt her work by becoming apprenticed to an older experienced midwife, and the local priest had to swear to the apprentice's good character. Throughout Europe in the Middle Ages it was the usual practice that women should be attended only by other women when giving birth.

Guides to women's health were written, to help midwives in their work. Some still survive today:

And so to assist women, I intend to write of how to help their secret maladies, so that one woman may aid another in her illness.

*Introduction to **A Medieval Woman's Guide to Health**, early 15th century, MS Sloane 2463*

The earliest known book on women's health and midwifery was written by Trotula of Salerno in the 11th century. At this time, Salerno in Italy was the most famous medical school in Europe, and at the height of its fame. Trotula is thought to have taught at the university, and her book, ***Diseases of Women*** gives evidence of her knowledge of general medicine and surgery of her day. Trotula made use of herbal remedies in the form of plasters and herbal baths. She wrote about the subject of women in labour:

It is helpful to a woman in difficult labour to be bathed in water in which has been cooked mallow, chickpeas, flaxseed and barley. Let her sides, abdomen and hips and flanks be rubbed with oil of violets. Let her be rubbed vigorously and let sugar and vinegar be given her to drink, and powdered mint and a dram of absinth. Let her sneezing be provoked by placing dust of incense in the nostrils, or powder of candisioum, or pepper.

*Trotula, **Diseases of Women**, 11th century*

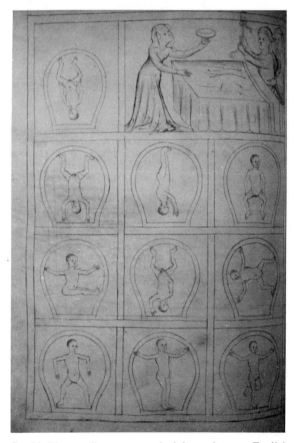

A midwife attending a woman in labour, from an English manuscript, c. 1400. It shows what were thought to be different possible positions of a baby at birth.

A woman surgeon performing a Caesarean section. Illustration from a French manuscript, c. 1375.

The growth of medicine as a profession

At the medical school in Salerno during the Middle Ages there were other women like Trotula who practised and taught medicine. The medical school was open to both men and women alike, although the number of women studying medicine was small. They were generally noble women or, like Calenda Costanza, were carrying on the work of their fathers. Calenda Costanza is mentioned in 1423, lecturing on medicine, and is said to have won special honours in her medical examinations.

Evidence of other women practising medicine in Italy comes from the licences issued by the City Authorities in Venice, Rome, Naples and Florence. One such licence, issued at the beginning of the 14th century, begins:

Since then, the law permitted women to exercise the profession of physician and since, besides, due regard being had to purity of morals, women are better suited to the treatment of women's diseases after having received the oath of fidelity, we permit . . . [name] . . .

In France and England, and in northern Europe generally, women were not allowed to study at university. It was the bishops rather than the City Authorities who issued licences to doctors. Nevertheless there is evidence of women practising medicine in England, even though they were not allowed to go to university. The evidence comes from sources such as monastic chronicles and parliamentary *rolls*. Here are details of women doctors from these sources:

Matilda, sage femme [wise-woman], Walingford, Berks. c. 1232
Matilda la Leche [leech, or healer], assessed this year 1232 at twenty pence.

This assessment was the amount of money Matilda had to pay in tax. It was much more than any other woman in the town, so she must have had a successful business.

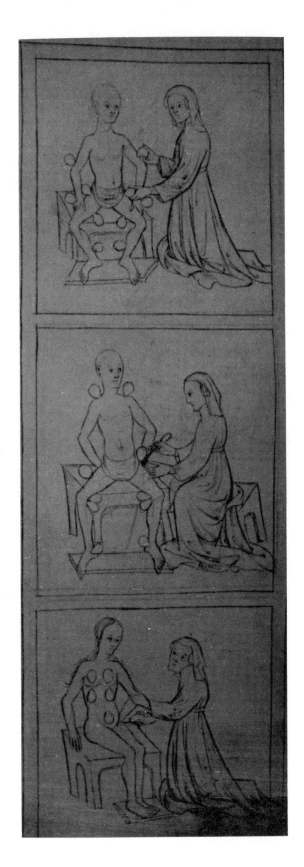

Physicians applying leeches (blood-sucking worms) to patients, in a widely accepted form of treatment known as blood-letting, or bleeding. Many ailments were thought to be caused by 'bad blood' and were treated in this way. Illustrations from an English manuscript c. 1400. Are the physicians and patients men or women?

Agnes, medica, Stanground, Hants. c. 1270

Agnes had an excellent reputation as a doctor. She appears in the records because she had a smallholding for which she had to pay the Abbot of Thorney two shillings each year.

Johanna, woman physician, Westminster, c. 1408

Johanna appears in the records of Westminster Abbey in 1407–8, where payment is recorded for various medicines for Brothers William Ashwell and Richard Merlow. She also appears the next year, when she was paid 3*s* 6*d* for medicine for Merlow. The fact that she is recorded as 'Johanna Leche' tells us that she was a doctor or healer, not an apothecary.

The disappearance of women doctors

From the late 14th century onwards, there is evidence which shows that there was strong opposition to women doctors. The work of the woman in the household, the wise-woman and the midwife continued, but those women who tried to practice medicine professionally met with a lot of hostility. This is what John Mirfield, a priest connected with St Bartholomew's Hospital in London thought of them:

. . . worthless and presumptuous women [who] usurp [try to take over] this profession to themselves and abuse it. Who, possessing neither natural ability, nor professional knowledge, make the greatest possible mistakes, thanks to their stupidity, and very often kill the patient.

John Mirfield, **Breviarium Bartholomei: the medical writings of a clerk at St Bartholomew's Hospital**, *c. 1370*

The case of Jacqueline Felicie De Almania, an unlicensed doctor in Paris, shows other arguments for and against women doctors at that time.

13

The case of Jacqueline Felicie De Almania

De Almania was brought before the Court of Justice in Paris in 1322, on the charge of illegally practising medicine within the city. She had no licence:

The said Jacoba visited the sick folk, labouring under severe illness in Paris and the suburbs, examining their urine, touching, feeling and holding their pulses, body and limbs. . . . After this examination she was want to say to the sick folk, 'I will cure you by God's will, if you will trust in me.' making a compact with them and receiving money from them.

Charter Paris II 257–58

The main witness for the prosecution was a surgeon, John of Padua, who at one time had been the surgeon to King Philip IV of France.

He pointed out that a law had been in existence for over 60 years which forbade women to practise medicine. Women, he argued, could not practise as lawyers, and so it was much more important that they be banned from medicine. This was because a woman doctor might kill a man, and this was surely more serious than losing a law suit?

De Almania was an extremely popular doctor because of her success with patients. Eight witnesses were called in her defence. Many of them said that she had succeeded in curing them when others had failed. In her own defence, De Almania argued that the law existed to stop ignorant women from practising medicine; it did not apply to women like herself who were knowledgeable doctors. She put the case for women doctors:

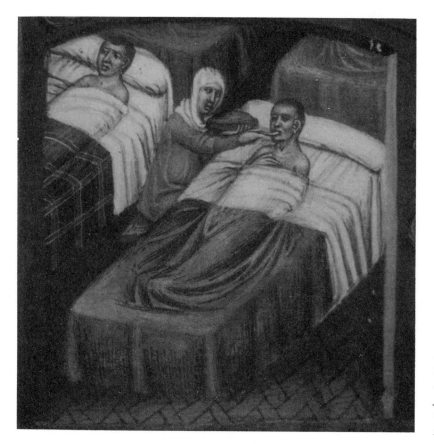

Nuns have always played an important part in caring for the sick. Some convents and monasteries had infirmaries for the sick attached to them. Here a nurse feeds a sick man. Illustration from a French psalter, (book of psalms), 15th century.

It is better and more seemly that a wise woman learned in the art should visit the sick woman and inquire into the secrets of her nature and her hidden parts, than that a man should do so, for whom it is not lawful to see and seek out the aforesaid parts, not to feel with his hands, the breasts, belly and feet of women. And a woman before now would allow herself to die, rather than reveal the secrets of her infirmities to a man . . .

Charter Paris II 257–58

Nevertheless, De Almania was found guilty. This is what the court decided:

Her plea that she cured many sick persons whom the aforesaid masters could not cure, ought not to stand and is frivolous, since it is certain that a man approved in the aforesaid art could cure the sick better than any woman.

Charter Paris II 257–58

She was found guilty, along with four other women who were also standing trial for practising medicine without a licence, and *excommunicated.*

Women did not give up their work as doctors that easily.

In England, this petition from a woman called Joan is further evidence that women doctors sought legal recognition:

To the very excellent and redoubtable, our very gracious lord the King. Your poor bedeswoman [a person asking a favour] Joan, formerly wife to William of Lee, prays very humbly that since her aforesaid lord was killed upon your first expedition to Wales whereof your aforesaid bedeswoman was left without support . . . and she has nought whereby to live save by physic, which she has learned, may it please your highness and most gracious lordship to grant to the aforesaid poor bedeswoman, a letter under your great seal, that she may go about the country safely to practise her art, without hindrance or disturbance from all folk, who despise her by reason of her said art . . .

Public Records Office, Ancient Petitions and File 231, c. 1404–8, No. 11510

We do not know if Joan was given the King's approval or not, but we are given a hint as to whom those who 'despise her by reason of her said art' might have been. In 1421 the doctors of physik petitioned Parliament, asking them to:

Limit the practise of fysyk [physik] to the scoles [schools] of Fisyk within some universities.

Rot. Parl. IV, p. 158

Their request was granted two years later, although it was difficult to enforce. Women healers did not disappear altogether, but the word 'physician' or 'doctor' rapidly became a word which described an exclusively male profession.

Two midwifes attending the birth of Christ, from an Italian manuscript, 14th century. Although the subject is biblical, the artist has used contemporary clothes and setting, which gives us an idea of what an upper-class birth scene may have been like in the 14th century.

3   Healing in the 16th, 17th and 18th centuries

Upper-class women healers

In the 16th and 17th centuries, women of all classes continued to play an important role as healers in the home. During this period the number of books on household management increased. These books were written for upper-class women and passed on advice and comments about the management of a large household. They had long sections on the treatment of illnesses and had prescriptions for cures.

In one such household book, *Character of a Good Woman*, a 'Good Woman' is described as someone who:

. . . distributes among the indigent [needy] poor money, books and clothes and Physik, as their several circumstances may require [and to relieve] her poorer neighbours in sudden distress, when a doctor is not [when there is no doctor], or when they have no money to buy what is necessary for them.

Roger Timothy, **Character of a Good Woman**, *1697*

The writer, John Evelyn, described the activities of his mother and sister when he was young:

Their recreation was in the distillorie, the knowledge of plants and their virtues for the comfort of the poor neighbours and the use of their family.

John Evelyn, **Diary**, *19 January 1686*

The opening pages of Hannah Wolley's book, The Accomplisht Ladys Delight, *1675. The picture shows Hannah Wolley (left) and women preserving food, making medicines, beautifying themselves and cooking (right).*

Anne, Countess of Arundel, turned her house into a hospital. It supplied:

. . . medicines and salves, plaster and other remedies to all kinds of people who are either wanting [lacking] will or means to go to doctors and Chirurgeons [surgeons] and came to her for the curing of their wounds and distempers.

H. G. F. Howard, Duke of Norfolk, **The Life of Anne Countess of Arundel**, *published 1857*

Some women like Hannah Wolley, published their work. Hannah wrote a book on diet and medicine for women, **Pharmacopolium Muliebris Sexus**, in 1674. The book was reprinted in 1688 and was translated into German. She wrote in her book that her mother and sister were 'well skilled in physic and surgery', and that she had learned from them.

Upper-class women throughout Europe did similar work. Their writings repeatedly say that daughters learned their knowledge from their mothers. Learning about medicine and cures was a normal part of the up-bringing of young girls of noble birth. The private diary of Lady Anne Clifford (born in 1590), describes her mother:

[She] was a lover of the study of medicine and the practise of Alchemy. She prepared excellent medicines that did good to many. She delighted in distilling waters and getting chemical reactions with her extracts.

Lady Clifford continued her mother's work and used the prescriptions to treat the sick people on her family's estates.

Knowing about herbal remedies was considered to be so important that herbalists were employed to give lessons:

July 5th 1674, by me to Bro [Brother] Lower, so that he might give Thomas Lawson for coming hither to instruct him and his sister in the knowledge of herbs . . . 10s

Sarah Fell, Account Book, 1674

Upper-class women would also read medical books written by the learned men of the day. Anthony Walker described Elizabeth Walker, who worked for Lady Warwick:

[She] was skilled both as a physician and surgeon . . . and she was very inquisitive of other doctors and

A drawing from Elizabeth Blackwell's book, A Curious Herbal Containing Five Hundred Cuts of the most Useful in the Practice of Physik, *1756. This herb rosemary is used in cooking, but infusions of it can be taken to improve blood circulation and to relieve nervous tension and colds.*

had many English books, Riveriusm, Culpeper, Bonettus etc. which she read.

Anthony Walker, **Holy Life of Mrs E. Walker**, *1690*

A changing role

Recipe books and books on household management began to change in the 18th century. After 1750, few of these books had sections on medicine. This reflects a change in the role of upper-class women in medicine.

At about the same time, books on home medicines appeared, written by university-trained doctors. This is typical of the tone of some of them:

In days gone by when men of rank spent most of their time in country mansions, the mistresses necessarily became the Lady Bountiful, and from preserving and pickling turned to the preparation of plasters, salves, surfeit waters. With much condescension, she visited and dispensed to the sick and charitably supplied all their wants. But now that there are parish officers to oversee the poor and charitable hospitals and dispensaries for the sick, it was time for the ladies to retire.

James Adair, **Medical Cautions***, 1786*

By the 18th century, few upper-class women were involved in medicine and healing. The reasons for this go back a long way:

- New ideas about medicine, anatomy and surgery were developed by the scholars in the universities. Men like Andreas Versallius (1514–1649), challenged the old ideas about anatomy which were based on the work of Hippocrates. These new ideas were based on the close observation and dissection of the human body. Women were unable to study anatomy in this way because they were not admitted to the universities.

- New and expensive cures were developed by apothecaries, using the drugs imported into Europe as a result of the expansion of trade between Europe and India, China and the New World. In 1567, £600 worth of drugs were imported into England. By 1670, this had risen to £60,000 worth. These drugs were handled by merchants and businessmen, surgeons and apothecaries, and were not easily available for women to use.

- The number of professional doctors began to increase, particularly outside London. Canterbury, a city with a population of around 2,000, had 22 doctors in 1700. By the end of the 18th century, there were very few market towns in England without a resident physician.

- More and more cases of illness were being referred to the university-trained physicians by the upper classes. It became a status symbol and a sign of wealth to employ a physician. This fashion spread and was followed by the growing merchant class.

A young woman consults the village wise-woman about an ailment. Local healers offered cures based on herbal remedies; they were derived from long experience as well as trial and error. Painting from the 18th century.

4 Witchcraft, magic and medicine

In 1512 an *Act* was passed in England which said that no-one could practise medicine unless that person was a graduate of Oxford or Cambridge University, or were examined by the Bishop of London or the Dean of St Paul's Cathedral, together with four doctors of Physik. This law was passed because of pressure on the King from the physicians, apothecaries and surgeons, who objected to:

... common artificers, [such] as smiths, weavers and women, boldly and customably take it upon them great Cures and Things of great difficulty in which they partly use Sourceries and Witchcraft, and partly apply such medicines unto the diseases as were very noyous [harmful].

Petition to Henry VIII, 1512

It was difficult to enforce this Act and it was seen to give too much privilege to the surgeons and physicians. Another Act, passed in 1542, removed some of the restrictions on medical practice, and enabled 'divers honest men and women' to carry on with their healing.

In that same year, however, the first law against witchcraft in England was passed: 'The Act against conjourors, and witchcraft and sourcery and enchantments' (1542). The Act said that witchcraft was no longer a matter to be dealt with by the Church Courts, but had become a serious criminal offence punishable by death.

Who were the witches?

In general the people accused of witchcraft were women. Many more women than men were accused of witchcraft and found guilty, as the table on page 20 shows. Between 1587 and 1593, for example, Archbishop Elector of Trier organised witch-hunts and burned 368 witches from 22 German villages. At the end of the witch-hunts, two of the villages were left with only one woman apiece. There were witch-hunts from time to time throughout Europe and America between the 15th and 18th centuries.

The biggest influence on people's thinking about witches came from the writings of two Dominican monks who worked for the Spanish *Inquisition*. In their book, **Malleus Maleficarum** (The Hammer of the Witches), they wrote that women, rather men, were likely to be witches. Women were seen as imperfect human beings and the Christian Church taught that women were the cause of

Newes from Scotland.

where immediatly she accused these persons following to be notorious witches, and caused them forthwith to be apprehended one after an

other, viz. Agnis Sampson the eldest Witch of them al, dwelling in Haddington, Agnes Tompson of Edenbrough, Doctor Fian, alias John Cunningham, maister of the Schoole at Saltpans

Illustration from Newes from Scotland, *1591, the first work on Scottish witchcraft. It shows Agnis Sampson, and three other women accused of witchcraft, being questioned by King James VI of Scotland. The King wrote a book on witchcraft himself, in which he explained why so many witches were women: 'for as that sex is frailer than man, so it is easier to be intrapped in these gross snares of the Devil, as was well proved by the Serpent's deceiving of Eve' (James VI,* Daemonology, *1597).*

bringing sin into the world and were therefore easy targets for the Devil.

Most of the women brought to trial, accused of witchcraft, were peasant women. With her apparent power of life and death, the village wise-woman seems to have been particularly open to accusations of witchcraft. The **Malleus Maleficarum** has a whole chapter on the witch-midwife who was to be feared:

For when they do not kill the child, they offer it to the devil in this manner. As soon as the child is born the midwife, if the mother herself is not a witch, carries it out of the room on the pretext of warming it, raises it up, and offers it to the Prince of Devils, that is Lucifer, and to all devils. And this is done by the kitchen fire.

Malleus Maleficarum, 1487

The fact that so many women were put to death as a result of the witch-hunts is important to our understanding of the position of women healers in this period.

List of convicted witches

Nos. of indict- ment	Assize	Prisoner's name	Nature of witchcraft	Notes	Sentence	Judges
3–5	1564 Essex Sum.	Elizabeth Lowys	person to d.	preg.	[Hanged]	Southcote, J., Gerard, G.
7	'' Surrey Winter	Eden Worsley	person to d.	rep.	[1 year]	'' Saunders, T.
11–13	1565 Kent Lent	Joan Byden	persons to d. & c.		[Hanged]	'' Gerard, G.
14	'' Surrey Sum.	Joan Gowse	bull to d.		[1 year]	'' ''
15	'' '' ''	Rose Borow	person to d.	rep.	?	'' ''
17	1566 Essex Sum.	Elizabeth Frances (1)	person	confessed	1 year	'' ''
18	'' '' ''	Agnes Waterhouse	person to d.	confessed	Hanged	'' ''
20	1567 Essex Lent	Alice Prestmarye	person		[1 year]	'' ''
23	'' '' Sum.	Alice Atrum	horse, pig		[1 year]	'' ''
24	'' Kent ''	Agnes Bennett	person to d.		[Hanged]	'' ''
25	'' '' ''	Cecilia West	person		1 year	'' ''
29–32	1569 Essex Lent	Alice Swallow	persons to d. & c.		[Hanged]	'' Wray, C.
35–37	'' Surrey Sum	Jane Baldwyn	'' ''	rep.	[1 year]	'' ''
43	1571 Kent Sum.	Ellen Peckman	person to d.		[Hanged]	'' Gawdy, T.
45–48	1572 Essex Lent	William Skelton	person to d.		[Hanged]	'' Monson, Robt.
46–48	'' '' ''	Margery Skelton	person to d.		[Hanged]	'' ''
49	'' '' ''	Katherine Pullen	'' ''		[Hanged]	'' ''
50	'' '' ''	Elizabeth Frances (2)	person		1 year	'' ''
53–54	'' Sussex Lent	Joan Usbarne	cattle to d.		[1 year]	'' Gawdy, T.
58–61	'' Essex Sum.	Agnes Francys	person to d.		[Hanged]	'' ''
62–64	'' '' ''	Agnes Steademan	person & c.		[1 year]	'' ''
66	1573 Herts Lent	Thomas Heather	invocation		?	'' Monson, Robt.
67–69	1574 Essex Lent	Alice Chaundeler	person to d.		[Hanged]	'' ''
72–74	'' Kent Lent	Alice Daye	'' ''	preg.	[Hanged]	'' ''
75–79	'' Essex Sum.	Cecilia Glasenberye	person to d. & c.		Hanged	'' ''
80–81	'' '' ''	Elizabeth Taylor	person to d.		Hanged	'' ''
82	'' '' ''	Alice Hynckson	cattle to d.		1 year	'' ''
85–86	'' Kent Sum.	Alice Stanton	'' ''		[1 year]	'' ''
88	1575 Surrey Lent	Thomas Heather	invocation		Hanged	'' Gawdy, T.
89–91	'' '' ''	Agnes Crockford	person to d.	preg.	[Hanged]	'' ''

Extract from a list of persons convicted of witchcraft, from the Records of Assize for the Home Circuit (Criminal Courts for the Counties of Essex, Surrey, Hertfordshire, Sussex, Kent and Middlesex)

Why were witches accused?

It might be thought that the woman healer and midwife were in danger of being accused of witchcraft because of the charms and ritual used in their treatments. But it is important to remember that healing and medicine in this period often involved the use of some magic and ritual.

Physicians as well as wise-women used charms and chanted prayers as part of their treatment.

The power of charms was accepted by some of the Fellows of the Royal Society, the scientific society set up in England in 1660, which included some of the most important scholars of the day. Even they accepted the power of sympathetic magic – the idea that in order to cure a wound from a sword or other weapon, you put the ointment on the weapon and not on the wound.

John Locke, who was a Fellow of the Royal Society, wrote this prescription for pains in the kidneys:

Take three stone quart jugs – fill them with the urine of the patient, stop them close, bury them in the yard underground, and lay a tile over them that earth may fall not close upon them.

John Locke, 1681

It was not so much the type of healing being practised by the wise-woman which laid her open to the accusations of witchcraft, but the fact that she was an unlicensed healer. People who practised medicine without a licence were sometimes accused of being witches because they were thought to have got their healing power from the Devil and not from God.

But it is important to note that not all the women accused oι witchcraft were healers, and not all healers were accused of witchcraft. There are many theories about why some women were accused of witchcraft. The one thing all the women who were brought to trial

Early 17th-century illustration showing the execution of witches in England. The man on the right is the witch-finder being paid.

as witches seemed to have in common was, 'the devilishe of her tonge'. Women who were particularly outspoken and critical of the way in which things were managed in their communities were likely to be accused of being a witch. They were brought to trial for:

. . . scolding and railing of most men, or rather every man when they do anything in the town's business or affairs contrary to her own mind, or not pleasing her, [and] for terming the parishoners to be a company of jackdaws.

Evidence from the Scottish Witch Trials, 17th century

The laws against witches were repealed in many countries in the 18th century. The last trial for witchcraft in England, for example, took place in 1712; and in Scotland in 1722. But by that time the witch-hunts had made it clear that the medicine of the physicians was accepted by the Church and State, whilst the medicine of the wise-woman was regarded as being based on superstition and ignorance.

The witch-hunts did not get rid of all women healers, only those who were seen as challenging the control of the State and Church. The Parish still employed women healers to treat the sick poor and to help at times of outbreaks of plague.

5 Everyday medicine in the 16th, 17th and 18th centuries

The plague

Between the 14th and 17th centuries there had been occasional outbreaks of the plague (Black Death) throughout Europe, although not all were as devastating as the famous outbreaks in England in 1347 and 1665.

In England the City Authorities employed women to do the unpleasant jobs associated with the plague. In 1592 it was agreed:

That in or for every parishe there shall be two sober ancient women, to be sworn to be viewers of the bodies of such as shall dye in time of infection.

Proceedings of the Court of Common Council, 1592

They worked as searchers, examining bodies for the black spots which were signs of the disease:

At this day, Mary Jerome widow, was sworn to be a searcher of all the bodies that shall die within the borough and they shall report and certify to her knowledge of what disease they died etc., and Anne Lovejoy, widow, jurata. 4 shillings a week a piece, allowing 4 shillings a month after.

Guilding, Reading Records, 1625

Women were employed during the outbreaks of plague to take care of the sick as well:

Agree to give widow Lovejoy in full satisfaction of all her paynes taken in and about the visited people in this Town in the last visitation [of the plague], 60 shillings in money, and cloth to make her kirtle and waistcoat.

Guilding, Reading Records, 1639

The Elizabethan Poor Law, 1601

These same women who dealt with victims of the plague were also paid to treat the poor who were sick, and to deliver the babies of pauper women. The Poor Law Act, passed by Queen Elizabeth, in 1601 meant that the sick poor had become the responsibility of the local parish. Before this Act, the poor were expected to fend for themselves. The Overseers of the Poor (parish officials) wanted to keep the cost of looking after the poor as low as possible, and so employed local wise-women, rather than pay the high fees demanded by university-trained doctors. The entries below

'Burying the dead' during the Great Plague in London, 1665, from a contemporary woodcut. The women walking in front of the coffin are searchers. In 1592 it was agreed, 'That in or for every parishe there shall be two sober ancient women, to be sworn to be viewers of the bodies of such as shall dye in time of infection' (Proceedings of the Court of Common Council).

are typical of those found in the parish account and *rate books* for the 17th and 18th centuries.

Item. To Mother Middleton for two nights watching with Widow Coxe's child being sick.

Hastings Documents, 1601

To Goody ['goodwife', the mistress of a house] Halliday, for nursing him and his family five weeks, £1.5 shillings: to Goody Nye, for assisting in nursing, 2 shillings and 6d. To Goody Peckham for nursing a beggar, 5 shillings. For nursing Wickham's boy with the small pox, 12 shillings.

Account Book of Cowden, 1704

Even when there was a hospital nearby, the parish accounts tell us that people were only sent there if they were very ill, as it was more expensive than employing the local wise-woman.

1737 April 16th. Paid to mother Simpson for a woman going to hang herself in Mr Booth's stable. 5.00d.

Paid to Mother Lack for looking after her 2s 6d May 9th.
Paid to mother Simpson for a woman that was sick 2s 6d.
1748 May 11th. Paid to Goody Cook for looking after the woman lying-in 10s 00d.
1764 Oct. 11th. Paid to Goody Sidding for looking after a poore woman when sick 1s 6d.

Church Warden's Accounts for the Parish of Lee, Lewisham, 1748

The Overseers of the Poor sometimes employed men to treat the sick poor. Men seem to have received more money than women for this service. The Poor Law Records for Marylebone in London include an entry of a payment to a midwife of 7s 6d for 'an extra ordinary case' of childbirth. In the neighbouring parish of Islington, The Overseers of the Poor record that a man-midwife was paid a guinea (£1 1s) for attending difficult labours (19 November 1731, 26 March 1756, 5 July 1756 and 26 August 1757).

A Drink for all Malignant Feavers.

I recommend unto you a Poffet drink to drink after it, wherewith I have cured many hundreds, in the time of the late unhappy Wars, of defperate Feavers Coufin (German to the *Plague*) which was then an *Epidemicall* difeafe, and ufed no other Medicine.

Take *Carduus Benedictus, Scabious* and *Butter-bur* roots, and boil them in poffet drink, and let them drink largely of it; and be not too fparing of your ingredients, for they are eafie enough to be had.

It may be objected, That it will be fo bitter you cannot drink it: To remedy that, boil it in the milk firft, and the longer it boils, the leffe bitter it will be; and when the bitterneffe is gone, ftrain it, and fet it on the fire again, and when it boils, put in your drink, and let it ftand to raife the curd, which take off.

This poffet drink hath ftayed violent *Vomitings* and *Loofeneffe*: by drinking largely of it many have been cured in 24 houres, when nothing but death hath been expected.

An outward Application for the Plague.

I will likewife give you an outward Medicine, as good as you fhall find in any fort compofed, which you may make your felves. Take *Bay-falt* if you can get it, and pound it fmall and burn it in a Firefho-vel till it leave crackling; if you cannot get *Bay-falt* take *White-falt*, and powder it very fine, then take *Caftle-fope*, flice it thin, and pound it in a Morter; adde to it as much oil of Lillies, as will make it foft to an oyntment, then take two parts of *Sope*, and one of *Figs*, and one of *Salt*, and another of *Mithridate*, and mix them together.

This will not deceive you in your expectation, for it will break any *Peftilentiall*

Cures for the plague from a page of a popular pamphlet, A Directory for the Poor against Infectious Disease, 1665.

6 Midwifery: the growing profession

Midwifery, like the other areas of medicine, came increasingly under the control of the Church in the 16th and 17th centuries. A law was passed in England in 1512, which stated that all midwives had to obtain a licence from the bishop before they could practise.

Under Church control

Below is an example of a midwife's licence. It was issued to Margaret Parrey on 30 August 1588 by John Aylmer, who was the Bishop of London:

John, by permission of God, Bishop of London, to our welle-loved in Christe margarett Parrey, widowe of the parishe of St Magnus in London . . . we have found you margaret apt, able and cunninge and experte to occupie and exercise the office, business and occupation of a midwife . . .

The licence then goes on to state how Margaret is to behave:

Ye shall be diligent and faithful and ready to help every woman travelling in Christ as well the poore as the rich, and that in time of necessity, ye shall not forsake the poor women and go to the rich . . . Ye shall neither cause nor suffer any women to name or put other father to the child but only him that is the very father indeed thereof . . . ye shall not in any wise use or exercise any manner witchcraft, charme, Sourcery invocations or other prayers than may be seem with godes Laws and the Queens

Midwifery becomes a profession

Until the 17th century nearly all midwives were women. But around 1625, a new phrase came into the English language: the man-midwife. By the mid-18th century, the *accoucheur*, as he preferred to be called, outnumbered the female midwives among the highly paid midwives employed by the upper class. (Among the lower classes, midwives were still mainly women.)

Here is some of the evidence which explains why and how this happened. You must remember that these changes took place very slowly over a period of 200 years.

The main change in the practice of midwifery in the 17th century, resulted from the invention of the delivery forceps by Peter and Hugh Chamberlain. The introduction of

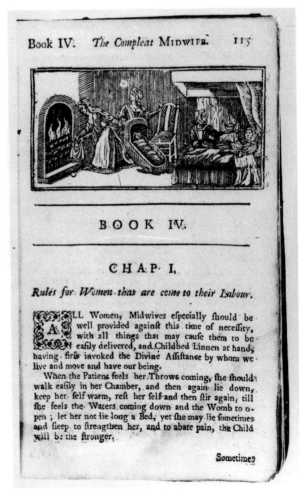

A page from The Compleat Midwife's Companion *by Jane Sharp, 1724.*

24

this new technology into childbirth paved the way for the man-midwife.

Sometimes in the case of a difficult labour, it was necessary to use surgical instruments to get the baby out. In England, under a law dating back to 1200, only people who were members of the Barber Surgeon Guild could use surgical instruments. Few, if any, midwives belonged to this Guild and so called in a surgeon to operate on these cases. Forceps were classified as surgical instruments and so few women midwives used them, whereas the man-midwife generally started out as a surgeon and so could use surgical instruments.

Forceps and the effects of the man-midwife

At first, many women in labour were reluctant to employ a man-midwife, because they only called in a man to help with the labour when some kind of surgery was necessary. They therefore associated men-midwives with difficult labour. Peter Willoughby (1596–1685), a man-midwife, was called in to assist his daughter, who was the midwife in this case, with a complicated labour. He recorded that he had to crawl into the lying-in room on all fours in order not to be seen by the woman patient (1658).

Some people also found the idea of a man-midwife shocking, and when he carried out his examination of the patient, she was covered with a sheet in order not to expose her body. This could not have been a very convenient or efficient way of working. Nevertheless, the man-midwife increased in popularity in the 17th century, particularly among fashionable society women. Using the new technology, he was regarded as being more effective than female midwives.

However, giving birth continued to be a very perilous process, even with the new technology. Whilst midwives with unwashed hands may have caused infections, so too did forceps, which at that time were not sterilised. If the forceps were not handled carefully, they could also tear and damage the mother and child. Because they were the latest fashion, forceps were often used unnecessarily. Although fewer women may have died in

The man-midwife. This etching advertises the English book The Man-midwife Dissected, *1793. What impression of the man-midwife is the artist trying to create? How does this compare with the woman-midwife?*

labour more may have died immediately after as a result of *sepsis* and *puerperal fever*.

We seldom hear of women dying in Labour, although many die in child-bed.

Blunt, ***The Man-midwife Dissected***, 1793

The man-midwife, with formal training in anatomy and surgery, was often highly critical of women as midwives. The man-midwife Peter Willoughby, for example, claimed that many midwives, particularly in the country areas, were:

. . . illiterate women of the meanest sort, who not knowing how to live otherwise, have taken it up for the getting of a shilling or two.

Observations in Midwifery, 1672

His definition of a good midwife was one who sent for a man to help with a difficult labour, and who was not, 'So lofty and conceited that she used the instruments herself.'

Delivery under a sheet. This woman is covered up whilst attended by a man-midwife, in order not to expose her body. Would this have affected the work of the man-midwife in any way? Illustration from a Dutch book by Janson, Korte en Bondige Verhandeling, *1711.*

Women midwives, on the other hand, often had more practical experience in midwifery. They were sometimes critical of the men-midwives and of their attempt to make midwifery into a profession, charging higher fees and giving it a higher social status. When Peter Chamberlain petitioned the King to form the midwives into a royal corporation, he was opposed by two other London midwives, Mrs Cellier and Mrs Whipp. They suspected Chamberlain of wanting to keep midwives ignorant, rather than encouraging them to improve their knowledge. Some midwives were badly trained and were encouraged to call in a man-midwife in cases of difficult labour:

. . . often times by their bungling and untoward usage of women and often times through ignorance, do send for him when it is none of his work . . . and do highly increase his profits.

Royal College of Physicians Annals, 1617

Chamberlain's petition was turned down by the enquiry into it by the Archbishop of Canterbury on the grounds that he had bribed other midwives to support his petition. The enquiry said that he did not have enough expertise since he did not attend normal deliveries, but only those 'where he could use his instruments'.

As the 17th century progressed, it became harder for women to learn about anatomy and how their bodies worked. Attitudes towards discussing anatomy changed. It was considered unnecessary and indeed vulgar for a woman to understand how her body worked. In the **Expert Midwife**, written in 1694, McMath said in his introduction that he did not include a:

description of the parts in a woman destined to Generation [i.e. her reproductive organs], not being absolutely necessary to this purpose, and lest it might seem execrable [offensive] to the more chaste and shamefaced through Bawdiness.

The idea that it was indecent for a woman to understand how her body worked became increasingly widespread as the upper-class woman left all matters of health to her doctor.

Women midwives were still far more numerous than men midwives, but the highly paid and prestigious jobs went to men. In 1726, Edinburgh town council appointed its first Professor of Midwifery – Joseph Gibson.

7 Smallpox: the development of inoculation

As a result of the work of the scholars and physicians working in the universities, people's knowledge of anatomy and *physiology* increased. Yet this knowledge did not mean medicine improved or that people had a longer life expectancy. In fact, the one 'invention' of the 18th century which did increase life expectancy – the use of inoculation against smallpox – had nothing to do with people's understanding of how the body worked.

Most people in Western countries will have been inoculated against smallpox and other diseases which can kill. Smallpox has now been declared extinct by the World Health Organisation. Yet in the 18th century and earlier the countries of Europe were frequently swept by epidemics of smallpox, which killed thousands of people. Smallpox caused fever, disfiguring skin eruptions, and very often death. It was highly contagious. But people who had the disease and survived were immune to re-infection: they never caught smallpox again.

The work of Lady Mary Wortley Montagu

The practice of smallpox inoculation first came to England from Turkey. Lady Montagu, a traveller and wife of the British Ambassador in Turkey, was largely responsible for introducing this unique form of medicine to England. She had observed the work of Turkish wise-women, who seemed to be able to prevent the spread of smallpox by giving people a mild dose of the virus.

The Letters of the Right Honourable Lady Mary Wortley Montagu, written during her travels into Europe, Asia and Africa (1735) tell us how she first came across inoculation against smallpox. On 1 April 1717, she wrote from Adrianople (Edirne), in Turkey:

. . . I am going to tell you a thing which will make you wish yourself here. The smallpox so fatal and general amongst us, is here entirely harmless, by the invention of engrafting which is the term they give it. There is a set of old women, who make it their business to perform the operation every autumn, in the month of September, when the great heat has abated. People send to one another to know if any of their family has a mind to have the smallpox; they make parties for this purpose and when they are met (commonly only 15 or 16 together) the old woman comes with a nutshell full of the matter of the best sort of smallpox and she asks what vein you please to have opened. She immediately rips open [the vein]

A section of a painting of Mary Wortley Montagu and her son, Edward, in Turkey, c. 1717.

27

that you offer her with a large needle (which gives you no more pain than a common scratch) and puts into the vein as much matter as can lie upon the head of her needle, and after that binds up the little wound with a hollow bit of shell, and in this manner opens four or five veins . . .

There is no example of anyone who has died of it, and you may believe I am well satisfied of this experiment, since I intend to try it on my dear son. I am patriotic enough to take pains to bring this invention into fashion in England and I should not fail to write to some of our doctors very particularly about it, if I knew any one of them that I thought had the virtue enough to destroy such a considerable branch of their revenue for the good of mankind.

Lady Montagu, Letter XXI

On her return to England, Lady Montagu began her campaign to introduce inoculation in England. She received support from Dr John Woodward of the Royal College of Surgeons. There is no doubt that people were more prepared to believe and trust a well-known doctor in such a matter than the wife of an ambassador. Their campaign was helped by the outbreak of a smallpox epidemic in 1721. In London 3,000 people died of the disease.

There were considerable dangers attached to inoculation, however. The smallpox virus increased in strength as it passed through the human body, so 'engrafting' carried a high risk of triggering epidemics. Children who had been inoculated could infect other people who had not been inoculated because they were carriers of the disease and, at that time no-one understood how the disease was passed on. There was also a great risk of causing other infections, especially infection of the brain, by this method.

A safer method: Jenner and the cowpox vaccination

Inoculation with smallpox matter was practised in a limited way for the next 70 years. It remained a dangerous thing to do, however. In 1796, Dr Edward Jenner devised a safer method of protecting people from the disease. Jenner experimented with inoculation using cowpox matter, having noticed that dairy maids who caught cowpox (a much less serious disease) rarely caught smallpox. Although at this time nobody could explain how it worked, vaccination against smallpox was very successful and paved the way for further understanding about the contagious nature of disease and immunisation.

A nurse vaccinating a child. Jenner's work was publicised throughout Europe. This illustration comes from a Spanish book on the use of vaccination, Origen y Descubrimiento de la Vaccina, *by Chaussier, 1801. Notice the items surrounding the woman and child. What do they convey?*

8 Public health in the industrial age

Snow's rents: an illustration from the magazine Health of Towns, *1847–8, showing the squalor of town life. How many health hazards can you see in this picture? What effect do you think the publication of this picture was supposed to have?*

The effects of industrialisation

With the invention of the steam engine and the power loom at the end of the 18th century, the mill and the factory rather than the home became the centre of manufacturing. People had to live near the new factories. Towns grew rapidly. For example, the population of Manchester trebled between 1773 and 1801. There was a severe shortage of housing. New houses were quickly built – poorly constructed, cramped, back-to-back buildings. There was no fresh water supply or sewerage system. Whole streets would share an earth closet which was rarely emptied. These conditions were to bring new hazards to people's health.

The cholera epidemic, 1831–2

Typhoid and tuberculosis thrived in the new, insanitary manufacturing towns. Then, in 1831, a new epidemic reached Britain through the port of Sunderland: cholera. This highly infectious disease had begun to move along the trade routes from Asia through Europe around 1818. There was no known remedy for the disease which swept through the crowded, dirty towns. By the end of 1832, as the first epidemic in Britain died down, some 21,000 out of a population of 14 million had died of cholera. The disease also had devastating effects in France, Spain, Italy and elsewhere in Europe during the 1830s. There were further outbreaks of the disease. In 1848 there were 72,000 deaths in Britain; in 1853 there were 30,000; and in 1866 there were 18,000.

Improving public health

In Britain, Parliament took no responsibility for supervising water supplies, sewerage, sanitation and health. But Local Boards of Health were set up in some towns as a result of the epidemic of 1831–2. However, they found it difficult to make ratepayers pay for improvements and maintenance of water and sewerage supplies in poor areas, despite the growing evidence that there was a link between the bad living conditions and the spread of disease. The Local Boards of Health were disbanded after the epidemic.

One of the most outspoken supporters of public health legislation was Edwin Chadwick. His main interest in this resulted from his work in the 1830s on the new Poor Law. He saw that one of the main causes of poverty was illness and therefore the poor rate could be reduced if towns were healthier places to live in. His *Report on the Sanitary Conditions of the Labouring Population of Great Britain* (1842) described the squalor and overcrowding in the industrial towns. He concluded that local government was responsible for causing insanitary conditions in the towns and that they were the people with

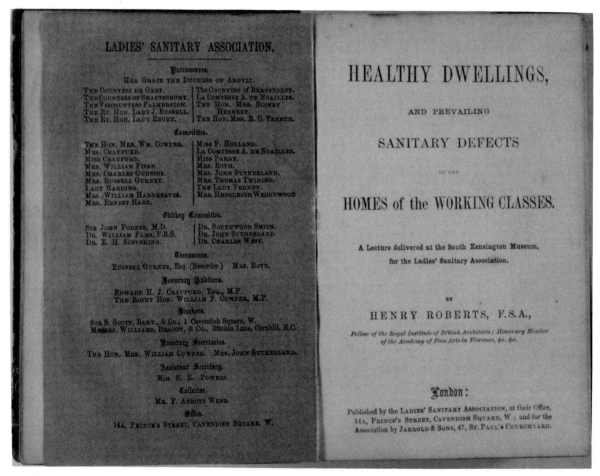

Opening pages of a pamphlet by the Ladies' Sanitary Association. This pamphlet campaigns for healthy homes for the working classes. Look at the list of patronnesses and committee-members. What do their names suggest?

the power to improve these conditions.

The government could not ignore Chadwick's findings and in 1848 Parliament passed the First Public Health Act, which set up a Central Board of Health for five years. Towns with a high death rate were forced to set up a Board of Health and appoint Medical Officers. Some towns did begin to make improvements to sewerage and water supplies, but others ignored the Public Health Act.

In 1858, the work of Dr John Snow added to people's understanding of the connections between lack of hygiene and disease. He made a study of the cholera cases in Westminster, London, and discovered that they had all used water from the same pump in Broad Street. This water was contaminated by sewerage from a house in which the people already had cholera. No action was taken by the government, though, to enforce public health provision.

Meanwhile, other people began to campaign for public health, using a slightly different approach.

The Ladies' Sanitary Association

Some upper and middle-class women decided to form the Ladies' Sanitary Association in 1858, to lead a campaign to improve public health. They argued that the work of reformers like Chadwick would only be effective if people were aware of good health in the home:

By some means or other, the grand political agencies of Parliament with their Acts and their Boards, must be narrowed down to minute domestic application. The cess pool . . . must not only be closed and got rid of . . . the chimney must be cured of smoking, the butcher must not sell bad meat. The infected clothes must be burned after an epidemic.

Ladies' Sanitary Association Annual Report, *1859*

As part of their campaign, they published *Tracts specially to the Poor*. In four years, they distributed 140,000 tracts on topics such as, *Health of Mothers, Cheap Doctors, Power of Soap and Water*, and *Worth of Fresh Air*.

Sanitary Inspectors

It was only after a third outbreak of cholera in 1865–6, that the government spelt out the responsibilities of Local Authorities towards the safeguarding of public health. Under the 1875 Public Health Act, *all* towns had to appoint a Medical Officer of Health and provide clean water, proper drainage and sewerage. Sanitary Inspectors were to report to the Medical Officer of Health on the actual conditions.

After 1875, many upper and middle-class woman began to contribute to improving public health by working at local government level as Sanitary Inspectors. We can get some idea of the work they did from the annual reports they wrote for the Medical Officers of Health. Frances Baker, a Sanitary Inspector for Marylebone in London, wrote the following report on 1 January 1909:

The following table gives a tabulation where tabulation is possible of my year's work:

Workshops re-inspected	88
New Workshops registered and measured	153
Visits respecting birth returns	1,009
Visits respecting phthisis [a wasting disease]	226
Visits respecting verminous schoolchildren	77
Visits respecting infectious diseases	43
Complaints received and investigated	63
Work in progress visited	25
Miscellaneous visits and Inspections	249

I am Sir,
Your obedient servant
Frances A. Baker

9 Medical care in the industrial towns

Public Health reform alone could not remove the ill-health which bred in industrial towns as a result of poverty, bad housing and low wages. It has been estimated that amongst the urban population in the mid-19th century, the number of cases each year of serious illness or injury was equal to about two-thirds of the total population. What medical treatment was available to people living in the industrial towns, and what happened to the women healers as a result of industrialisation?

The New Poor Law, 1834

In 1834, the Poor Law of 1601 (see page 22) was amended. Now parishes were to join together to form Unions to provide relief for the poor. This affected the medical treatment available to them. The Union surgeon now replaced the Parish surgeon. He served a much larger population and was paid much less per unit of population. What was more, he was usually expected to supply drugs and equipment out of his salary.

Due to the stigma attached to poverty, particularly under the New Poor Law, only a minority of the sick poor received their treatment from the Union doctor. The Committee on Medical Poor Relief (1844) estimated that in the manufacturing city of Leeds, only 1.4% of the population received poor relief. Evidence from the *First Report from the Commissioners on the Poor Law* in 1834 said that most people relied on household cures or the dispensing chemist.

Reconstruction of a typical chemist's shop in the late 19th century. As well as buying ready-made medicines, many women bought drugs like iodine and morphine over the chemist's counter, and made their own medicines at home. This shop was one of many owned in central England by the firm Bates and Hunt.

Household cures and women healers

For most working-class families, medical treatment still began in the home. By the mid-19th century there was a whole range of manufactured patent medicines to treat the sick which could be bought over the chemist's counter. These contained drugs like iodine, morphine, strychnine and quinine. Rather than pay out to buy these patent medicines, people bought the drugs at the chemist's and made up the medicines at home.

Favourite cures using these drugs were shared between women, and they had recipe books containing cures for coughs and headaches, alongside those for parkin and Victoria sponge cake. The drugs used in these cures were far more dangerous than the herbal remedies found in the 16th century cookery books. Laudanum, for example, is an addictive drug which when taken in large doses will kill. *The English Woman's Journal* recorded that in one district in Manchester in 1859, nineteen gallons of laudanum were sold each week by the three local chemist shops.

The recipe below comes from Annie Lamb's recipe book and dates from around 1880. Medicines like these may have had hazardous effects on some patients:

Westfield cough medicine

One penny worth of aniseed.
One penny worth of peppermint.
Laudanum.
½ lb. black treacle.

Pour one pint of boiling water onto the treacle, when nearly cold, add the other ingredients. Put in a bottle and shake. To be taken with water.

Yet with the absence of professional medical attention for the working class, these patent drugs and treatment by the local wise-woman were the only cures available. Conditions in the industrial towns made it increasingly difficult for the wise-woman to work and to keep up-to-date with medical practice. In the overcrowded tenement blocks of Leeds, Manchester, Liverpool, London and Glasgow, there were no back gardens in which to grow herbs for medicines. Special trips had to be made to the countryside to gather them. In a novel about industrial Manchester, Mrs Gaskell describes Alice Wilson:

She had been out all day in the fields gathering wild herbs and medicines, for in addition to her invaluable qualities as a sick nurse and her worldly occupation as a washer woman, she added considerable knowledge of hedge and field simples.

Mrs Gaskell, **Mary Barton***, 1848*

Despite these difficulties, wise-women were relied upon well into the 1920s and 1930s. The following extracts about Bristol at this time are written down from interviews (oral evidence):

Bertha Milton You never had a doctor unless you paid him. We never had a doctor. If you were ill mother rubbed your chest or put something in your ear. I never remember a doctor coming to our house.
Ralph Bewley You used to go down the Herbalist, down Stapleton Road.
Sid Stephens I lived in Salisbury Street – it was a street of good neighbours. I well remember one lady 'Grannie Hedges', she was the street 'doctor'. Any young mother who had illness, especially with children, she could tell what was wrong and could give advice free. A doctor's fee was 3s if you called to see him and if he had to call it was a charge of 6s, a lot of money in those days.

Bristol As We Remember It*, 1978*

These women were the same ones called upon to help deliver babies:

Oh, I think we managed. Martha used to come, the midwife, and they used to stop in bed a week in them days. She wasn't certified or anything, but she was one of the good old midwives and it was only a few shillings for a confinement.

Interview in Elizabeth Roberts, **A Woman's Place***, 1984*

In 1902, the Midwives Act required all people calling themselves midwives to be registered. It laid down qualifications for midwives. People still carried on using the unqualified midwives because they were cheaper to employ (between 5s and 7s 6d for an unqualified midwife, compared with 12s 6d and 17s 6d for a qualified one).

Doctors were no better trained in delivering babies than midwives were. Throughout the 19th century the death rate of women in childbirth was slightly higher amongst upper- and middle-class women who were attended by a doctor, than amongst working-class women attended by a midwife. A report published by the Scottish Board of Health in 1928, for example, found that the death rate among home deliveries attended by doctors

34

was 6.9 per 1,000, compared with 2.8 per 1,000 for home deliveries carried out by midwives.

A wise-woman was called in for other treatments too, though they did not always produce the desired result:

An enquiry was held on Tuesday [13 December] at the Green Man Inn, before Mr. Coroner Chaston, relative to the death of Maggie Alderton Wade, aged 1 year and 9 months, the child of Henry Wade, agricultural labourer. The evidence of the mother showed that the deceased accidentally overturned upon herself, last Friday, a boiling cup of soup, sustaining scalds from which she died 40 hours later. No medical man was called in but Mrs Brundish was sent for to charm the fire out of the deceased; she attended and repeated some words and passed her hands over the injured places. In the opinion of the parents of the deceased good was done. The witness added that Mrs Brundish's power was generally believed in, in the village. Mr Cuthbert, surgeon, having given evidence, a verdict of 'accidental death' was returned.

Suffolk Times and Mercury, *16 December 1892*

Women healers also became associated with practising criminal activities. In 1803 the Abortion Act made abortion illegal in Britain. Abortion had been one form of contraception used at a time when other methods were unknown or unavailable. In interviews with women who recalled family life at the beginning of this century, the historian Elizabeth Roberts found that 'abortion is discussed more often by respondents (the woman she interviewed) than mechanical contraception'. She writes:

It is possible . . . it was the former [i.e. abortion] which was the more usual way of limiting families in Preston before the Second World War.

Elizabeth Roberts, *A Woman's Place*, *1984*

It is difficult to get figures on abortion rates because it was an illegal activity, but it does seem that it was used by working-class women as one way of limiting the size of their families. According to the National Birthrate Commission in 1916, 25% of working-class women attempted abortion at one time or another. It is likely that they would turn to women healers for advice on this matter.

Abortion, carried out in back streets, was certainly much more dangerous than abortions carried out under proper medical supervision. Horror stories abounded about failed abortions:

I asked what this woman had used. She said it was like a stick and it is called slippery elm bark and it was sharpened at the end. When they got her to hospital they got it out of her, who had done it. It was like a sharp pencil at the end and they pushed it right up.

Interview with Mrs Dobson in Roberts, *A Woman's Place*, *1984*

The back-street abortionist continued to be in demand until abortion was made legal in Britain in 1967. Abortion has been made legal in other countries too: for example it was legalised in the USA in 1973, in Spain in 1975, and in France in 1976. It remains a controversial issue.

In Britain, effective medical treatment for all only became available when it was provided free of charge. This was achieved after the setting up of the National Health Service in 1947. The services of the wise-woman and domestic remedies were no longer needed.

By this time, however, the campaigns of middle-class women to go to university to study medicine and become qualified doctors had been successful, as the next chapter shows.

In the late 19th century, many advertisements for patent medicines appeared in newspapers and magazines. This is for the 'Carbolic Smoke Ball', a 'new American remedy'. It lists the names of the nobility who used it.

10 Women doctors in the 19th and 20th centuries

Women campaign to become doctors

Elizabeth Blackwell was registered as a doctor by the British Medical Association (BMA) in 1859. She had qualified in the USA and had come to Europe to continue her studies in Paris and London.

In the following year, the BMA changed its rules, and allowed only those people who had studied at a British university to become registered doctors. This new ruling effectively excluded women, because they were not allowed to study at British universities.

Elizabeth Blackwell did everything she could to encourage other women to train as doctors, but she recognised that this would not be easy. She wrote:

Society has not yet recognised this study as fit for women's work. Gossip and slanders may annoy the student and want of confidence on the part of women, with the absence of social and professional support and sympathy, will inevitably make the entrance of the young physician into medicine, a long and difficult struggle.

The English Woman's Journal, *January 1860*

Elizabeth Garrett Anderson was also determined to become a doctor. She spent some time training as a nurse and attended some of the lectures given to the medical students at the Middlesex Hospital in London, until the male students objected to her presence and insisted on her leaving. She was unsuccessful in all her applications for university courses, so she eventually studied privately with professors, took a course in midwifery and was given a qualification by the Society of Apothecaries. This enabled her to run a dispensary for women. She was able to take her final medical examination in Paris (in French of course), and this, with the licence from the Society of Apothecaries, allowed her to practise as a doctor in 1870.

Other women following in Elizabeth Garrett Anderson's footsteps were unable to

Elizabeth Garrett Anderson (1836–1917): the first woman to qualify as a doctor in Britain.

qualify in the same way. After she had obtained her licence from the Society of Apothecaries, they passed a resolution forbidding students from receiving private tuition for their examination. In future, candidates for their diploma must have worked in a recognised medical school. Women were excluded from these. The campaign then began for women to be admitted to university medical schools on the same terms as men.

Sophia Jex Blake, along with Edith Pechy, persuaded Edinburgh University to let them into medical lectures. Here, the women faced a great deal of opposition and harrassment from the other medical students. During their second year, they were refused permission to do the practical work in the Infirmary, and then the medical students tried to get them thrown out of the anatomy examination.

On the afternoon of Friday 18th November 1870, we women walked to the Surgeon's Hall. As soon as we came to the Surgeon's Hall, we saw a dense mob filling up the road in front . . . Not a single policeman was visible though the crowd was sufficient to stop all the traffic for an hour. We walked up to the gates, which remained open until we came within a yard of them, when they were slammed in our faces by a number of young men.

Sophia Jex Blake, **Medical Education of Women,** *1878*

Having taken their examinations, the women walked home whilst the male students hurled mud and insults at them.

Despite public sympathy for the women's cause, Edinburgh University would only give them a Certificate of Proficiency at the end of the course. They had taken the same examination as the men who were awarded degrees. The Certificates were not recognised by the BMA.

The women's situation was brought before Parliament. The University's decision had prompted a debate in the pages of the newspapers and journals of the day. William Cowper Temple was sympathetic to the

Students at Cambridge University protesting against women obtaining degrees, 1897. The banner reads: 'Here's no place for you maids . . .'

campaign for women to become doctors and, supported by Russell Gurney, introduced a *Bill* in 1875 to enable universities to educate and graduate women on the same terms as men. The Bill received a lot of public support, including 65 petitions in its favour. One petition was signed by 16,000 women; one was signed by the Edinburgh lecturers who had taught the women: and another was from 23 Professors of the Scottish Universities. Only 4 petitions were received against it. The Act allowing women to go to university and become doctors was eventually passed in August 1876.

In the USA the male medical schools also began to open their doors to women at the end of the 19th century, and by 1894, women made up about 10% of the students at 18 medical schools run by men in various American states.

Women doctors: the arguments

The Lancet and *The English Woman's Journal* both carried articles on whether women should be allowed to become doctors. Some men felt that women were not physically capable of doing the work:

I believe most conscientiously and thoroughly that women as a body are sexually, constitutionally and mentally unfit for the hard incessant toil, and for the heavy responsibilities of general surgical practice. At the same time, I believe as thoroughly that there is a branch of our profession – midwifery – to which they might be admitted in a subordinate position as a rule.

Dr H. Bennett, **The Lancet**, *June 1870*

The idea of women doing hard physical work may have been an alien idea to the image of middle-class Victorian women, but these women knew that their sex was quite capable of hard physical work:

I have myself been told by an eyewitness, that in Staffordshire, women are doing, 'not men's work, but horse's work', and it is an unquestionable fact that the low, rough and exhausting work is given over to them.

From correspondence discussing women doctors, **The English Woman's Journal**, *1862*

A common argument against women training to be doctors was that men would be embarrassed to be treated by them. It was readily answerable:

More than half of the ordinary medical practice lies among women and children . . . At present, when women need medical aid or advice, they have to go out of their world as it were; the whole atmosphere of professional life is so entirely foreign to that in which they live that there is a gap between them and the physician whom they consult, which can only be filled by making the profession no longer an exclusively male one.

Drs Elizabeth and Emily Blackwell, **The English Woman's Journal**, *1860*

Nursing: respectable work for women

At the same time that women were campaigning to train as doctors, other women were contributing to the rise in medical standards in Britain through their efforts to

Florence Nightingale: she fought doggedly for improvements in nursing and sanitation.

improve nursing. By the 1860s, some hospitals began to recognise that good nursing played an important part in a patient's treatment and they gave medical training to their nurses. The popular image of a nurse as a woman who was, 'too old, too weak, too drunken, too dirty, too stolid or too bad to do anything else' (in Florence Nightingale's words), was being overturned by the trained, skilled and competent nurses emerging from the new teaching hospitals. The most famous of these was the Nightingale Training School, founded in 1860 and attached to St Thomas' Hospital in London.

Florence Nightingale is remembered as the pioneer who made nursing respectable work for women. She came from an upper-class family and had to fight against their disapproval of her becoming a nurse. The Crimean War (1854–5) turned Florence Nightingale into a national heroine. In the Crimea she set up an efficient and effective military hospital to nurse the sick and wounded soldiers.

Meanwhile Mary Seacole, a black doctor from Kingston, Jamaica, also offered to go to the Crimea to nurse the troops. She had an extensive medical knowledge and nearly 30 years of practical experience in treating people with cholera and typhoid fever.

She came to England in 1854 to apply to go out to nurse in the Crimea. Although she had problems being accepted for a post, she was very determined, and in the end got to the Crimea by paying her own passage. She set up 'The British Hotel', two miles from Balaclava:

Before very long, I found myself surrounded with patients of my own . . . I was very familiar with the diseases which they suffered most from and successful in their treatment.

Mary Seacole, *The Wonderful Adventures of Mrs Seacole in Many Lands*, 1856

When the war ended, Mary Seacole returned to England and wrote her autobiography, *The Wonderful Adventures of Mrs Seacole in Many Lands*. She soon became a household name and received much public acclaim. In 1867, the Seacole Fund, supported by, among others, Queen Victoria, was set up to care for her in old age.

Mary Seacole: she used her extensive medical knowledge and nearly 30 years' practical experience in treating cholera and typhoid fever to help patients in the Crimea.

Until recently, her book and the work she did in the Crimea, have been ignored by historians. The Crimean veterans whom she had treated were anxious that she should not be forgotten. One of them wrote to *The Times*:

While the benevolent deeds of Florence Nightingale are being handed down to posterity with blessings and imperishable renown, are the . . . actions of Mrs Seacole to be entirely forgotten, and will none now testify to the worth of those services of the late mistress of Spring-hill?

The Times, April 1857

Florence Nightingale used her friends and contacts in the government to convince the public and the Medical Officers of the necessity for good nursing. Following her return from the Crimea, she spent the rest of her long life advising politicians and Medical Officers on matters of public health and hospitals, and overseeing the setting up of training hospitals.

11 The effects of war on medicine

Women doctors and the First World War

In September 1914, Dr Kathleen MacPhail wrote to the British War Office asking for permission to go and work in France. She received this reply:

Madame,
  I am directed to inform you that the employment of lady doctors with the forces is not to be contemplated.

Diary of Dr MacPhail, Imperial War Museum

Although women could now study medicine at university (since 1876) and practise as doctors, they were not allowed to go to the front.

The War Office had already been approached by Dr Elsie Inglis, who had been inspired to become a doctor by Sophia Jex Blake. After qualifying, Dr Inglis had founded a free hospice for women and children in the Edinburgh slums. When war broke out, she raised £25,000 in one month to set up the

Dr Elsie Inglis in uniform. The Scottish Women's Field Hospitals, set up in Serbia by Dr Inglis and Dr MacPhail, tackled the typhoid epidemic which had broken out. Dr Inglis' hospital was captured by the Austrians, and she and her patients were taken into captivity.

Scottish Field Hospital, staffed by all-women teams, including surgeons, chauffeurs and orderlies. She offered this to the War Office, and received the reply, 'Go and sit quietly at home dear Lady.'

Dr Inglis explained the position to Dr MacPhail:

The War Office will not send any women doctors to the front. They have definitely told us so. The *Scottish Federation of Women's Suffrage Societies* [a federation campaigning for votes for women] is going to organise hospitals which will be sent out under either the French or Belgian Red Cross, or to Serbia, where they are in great need of medical help.

Letter from Dr Inglis to Dr MacPhail, 1914

In December 1914, Dr Inglis and Dr MacPhail set off for Serbia with the first Scottish Women's Hospital Unit.

Another Scottish woman doctor, Dr McNeill, was sent to the Scottish Women's Hospital Unit in Salonika (then in the Ottoman Empire, now Thessaloniki in Greece). She described the hospital unit in her diary:

A long low shed, divided, we find on entering, with two compartments, an operating theatre and an X-ray room. The operating theatre is surprisingly well arranged and there is a good array of instruments . . . The X-ray is skilfully managed and proves invaluable assistance in diagnosis and in the location of bullets and shrapnel.

Diary of Dr McNeill, 21 October 1916

Although the Scottish Women's Hospital Unit had nothing to do with the British government, and indeed had been organised because the War Office had rejected women doctors, the War Office announced in December 1916 that the Unit had been 'given' to the Serbian government:

This morning, Dr McIlroy told us that the British War Office had 'given' us to the Serbs. But General Ruart has arranged that whilst we remain in Salonika we are a French unit, admitting, however, only Serbs. When we more up country, we shall be a unit of the Serbian army. It seems the British promised the Serbs 7,000 beds, of which our 300 are now reckoned part.

Diary of Dr McNeill, 7 December 1916

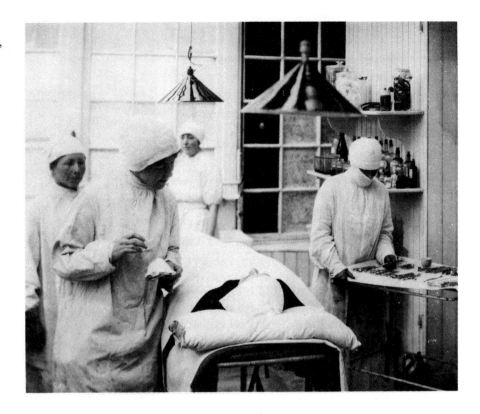

Female surgeon, Dr Robertson, and anaesthetist, Dr McNeill, working at the Women's Hospital at Chateau Mauritien, Wimereux, in France.

By 1916 the War Office had, in fact, changed its attitude to women doctors and had begun to recruit them for service abroad. By the end of the war, 150 women doctors served under the War Office in Britain. These included 85 in Malta, 36 in Egypt, 21 in France and 39 in Salonika. Yet these women doctors, unlike the men, were not given commissions. This brought home the fact to women doctors that although in many cases they were more experienced than the men, they were not thought capable of shouldering responsibility.

The work of the Medical Women's Federation

This attitude led directly to a campaign, which continued even when the war ended, to obtain the same recognition for women doctors as there was for men. The campaign was led by the Medical Women's Federation. In its newsletter it explains:

The War Office has succeeded in setting up a precedent that medical women, though equally qualified with medical men, and though doing the same work, yet rank as inferior to them. The granting of commissions now, would not only be the best way in which the War Office could show its appreciation of the work that medical women have done in the Army, but it would prevent the government from ever using the precedent to the detriment of medical women.

Medical Women's Federation, **Newsletter**, *1919*

The need for women doctors in the war certainly made it easier for women to train as doctors. Hospitals such as King's College Hospital and University College Hospital in London, which until 1915 had only accepted men, began to train women.

The figures in the table (page 42) show how the number of women training to be doctors increased throughout Britain around this time.

The war did not only make it easier for women to be accepted by the medical hospitals; they also learnt new skills. Their knowledge of surgery, and epidemic diseases like typhoid and cholera, increased. They contributed to the new knowledge which the treatment of war wounds and gassed soldiers demanded.

Numbers of doctors qualifying

Year	No. of women	No. of men
1917	78	539
1918	68	341
1919	99	175
1920	210	374
1921	602	325

Note The students graduating in 1921 would have begun their training during the war in 1916–17.

British Red Cross, 24 October 1921

The front-line nurses

As the war casualties flooded the hospitals, there was a great demand for nurses to cope with the wounded soldiers. No official register of trained nurses existed in 1914, so it was difficult for the government to recruit nurses. Many trained nurses volunteered for war work and were organised by the Red Cross. Other women became *VADs* (Women's Voluntary Aid Detachment) and were sent to work in British hospitals and to field hospitals in Allied Europe.

Some of the nurses who were sent to France have left a record of their activities in their letters and diaries. Millicent Peterkin, for example, served as a Red Cross Sister in France. She was mobilised on 14 August 1914 and sent to a Field Hospital in France, near Nantes. It took at least nine days for the wounded soldiers from the trenches to get to the hospital. She wrote in her diary:

It seems so absurd to keep hospitals partly shut up away down here when they are so badly needed at the front.

Diary of Millicent Peterkin, 27 September 1914

Many of the soldiers died from *sepsis* and *gangrene* that set in on the way to the hospital.

Some doctors worked in the trenches on the front line. In August 1914, a flying ambulance corps, which included four women, was organised to assist the Belgian army. Two of the women in the corps, Maria Chisholm and Elsie Knocker, carried medical supplies to the trenches on motor bikes. Later the two women

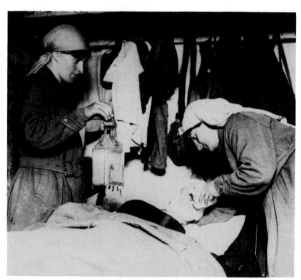

Marie Chisholm and Elsie Knocker, the 'Women of Pervyse', attending to wounded soldiers at the Front in northern France.

set up a hospital on the front line at Pervyse.

Thousands of women joined the VADs, but they were not encouraged to be more than hospital helpers. The fear of thousands of VADs flooding back to work in hospitals after the war, probably explains why, in 1919, the British government passed the Nurses Registration Act, which laid down the minimum age and qualifications to become a State Registered Nurse.

12 Women in medicine today

On the same terms as men?

In the mid 1980s, nearly half the students entering medical schools in Britain were female. The number has increased since the passing of the Sex Discrimination Act of 1977. This ended the quota system under which medical schools had allocated the majority of places to men and the minority to women. The number of women doctors in general practice and the hospital service almost doubled between 1974 and 1984.

Women doctors working in the health service

Area of work	1963	1974	1983
Hospital service	2,474	4,407	7,790
Community health service	not applicable	2,228	3,511
General medical service	1,746	2,975	4,876
TOTALS	—	9,610	16,177

House of Commons, 'Written Answer', 22 March 1984

Number of General Practitioners (family doctors) in Britain, 1985

Male	20,714
Female	5,476

Health and Personal Services Statistics, DHSS April 1987

Although more women are becoming doctors, the number appointed to senior positions is still proportionately low. In 1984, only 12% of *consultants* and 3.3% of surgeons in Britain were women. But the increase in the number of women doctors should eventually result in more women being appointed to senior positions in medicine.

The Medical Women's Federation which campaigned for the recognition of women doctors after the First World War (see Chapter 11), continues today to campaign for the interests of women doctors. In 1986 its President, Dr Beulah Bewley, commented on the differences between women and men doctors:

Women doctors, like women in general, still bear the major burden of household responsibilities which make it more difficult for them to work in the more competitive branches of medicine.

MWF Conference, 1986

This is how two women who have made it to the top of the medical profession see their work.

Professor Dame Sheila Sherlock is a leading authority on liver disease, Professor of Medicine and Honorary Consultant Physician at the Royal Free Hospital in Hampstead, London. She is not a member of the MWF and disagrees with many of their aims.

I think we ought to fight on merit alone. I'm not a feminist and I don't believe a woman has to be better than a man to succeed – just better than the best . . .

Professor Dame Sheila Sherlock, 1985

Dr Lotte Newman is a doctor in London and the current Honorary Secretary of the Medical Women's Federation. She is the only elected woman member on the Council of the Royal College of General Practitioners. She believes that medicine is still male-dominated – to the patients' cost.

It's not just because women drop out to have babies, they're just not appointed. Why? Because there are so few women on the college councils making selections. Women doctors have a lot to offer and they do practise in a different way. They tend to be less arrogant and authoritarian, more intuitive, more inclined to listen – especially in regard to women's problems and in bridging the language and cultural barriers.

Dr Lotte Newman, 1985

The effect of women doctors on medicine

Because there are more women in medicine today, there is an increasing awareness of women's health and healthcare. It is now widely recognised that the medical care needed by women and men will often be different. The different life-styles of women and men produce different illnesses, one obvious example being the higher rate of lung cancer and coronary disease among men. Different biology produces different medical needs (eg. pregnancy).

Pressure groups outside the medical profession have also been set up to make women's health needs more explicit. One such group is the Women's National Cancer Control Campaign which is campaigning for earlier and more effective screening of cervical and breast cancer. The National Childbirth Trust campaigns for the right of women to decide on the method of childbirth. This campaign has had the effect of raising the wider question of the role and rights of the patient in medical treatment.

There is a growing awareness among people in general that medicine and doctors do not offer 'miracles'. Some illnesses cannot be cured despite the advances in medical research. This awareness is leading people, and perhaps women especially, to learn more about their own bodies to prevent illness and maintain health.

A woman surgeon today. Pauling Cutting is a Fellow of the Royal College of Surgeons and performs general surgery. Her recent medical work in a besieged refugee camp in Beirut, Lebanon, has earned her worldwide recognition.

Questions

1
i) What problems do historians face when trying to find out about a past civilisation like that of Ancient Egypt?

ii) Look at the cure for a headache on page 6. What does it tell us about Ancient Egyptian medicine?

iii) What evidence is there about the part women played in medicine in Ancient Greece?

iv) Read the Roman Tombstone inscriptions on pages 8 and 9. What aspects of the women's lives do they mention first? What do these inscriptions suggest about attitudes to women and women's lives in Roman times?

2
i) What do the extracts from the Paston Letters (page 10) tell us about medicine and healing in the 15th century?

ii) Read the extracts from John Mirfield (page 13), the trial of De Almania (page 14), the Petition from Joan (page 15), and the Petition to Parliament in 1421 (page 15). What impression does John Mirfield's evidence give you of women healers? What do the other pieces of evidence add to our understanding of doctors in the Middle Ages?

3
i) Look at the extracts from the Scottish Witch Trials on page 21. What words are used to describe the accused women? What does this suggest to you about witchcraft?

ii) Does the fact that the Fellows of the Royal Society believed in sympathetic magic add to our understanding of 17th-century medicine?

4
i) What does the licence issued to Margaret Parrey (page 24) tell us about 16th-century midwifery?

ii) Look at the picture of the man-midwife on page 25. Does the cartoonist favour men-midwives or attack them? Give reasons for your answer.

iii) What information does a historian need in order to work out whether the use of forceps produced an improvement in the methods of childbirth, or not?

5
i) Who, according to the evidence in Chapter 7, first used inoculation against smallpox?

ii) Some people argue that Lady Montagu did not make much of a contribution to help stop the spread of smallpox. Draw two columns on a sheet. Head one 'For Lady Montagu' and the other 'Against Lady Montagu'. Using the evidence in the chapter, write down points for and against her.

6
i) Most history books on public health mention the work of Edwin Chadwick. Why do you think they do not mention the Ladies' Sanitary Association too?

ii) What was the difference in approach to the problems of public health between Chadwick and the Ladies' Sanitary Association? Why do you think they used different methods of campaigning for better health?

iii) Using Frances Baker's Annual Report (page 31), work out which areas of public health were the responsibility of the local government at the turn of the century. What aspects of public health are missing from this report?

7
i) What changes took place in domestic medicine in the industrial towns and cities in Britain in the 19th century?

ii) To find out about the lives of ordinary people, historians may interview them.

What do you think are the advantages and disadvantages of this kind of 'oral history'? Is it more or less reliable than other sorts of historical evidence? Explain your answer.

iii) Why is it so difficult for historians to get accurate figures on abortion rates in the 19th century? How do they manage to get any evidence at all?

8 i) What do the arguments used against women becoming doctors in the 19th century tell you about people's attitudes to women at that time?

ii) Who were the people who put forward arguments against women doctors and why did they do it?

9 i) What effects did the First World War have on women working in medicine?

ii) Imagine you are Dr Kathleen MacPhail. The year is 1919. Write a letter to *The Times* explaining what part women doctors played in the war. Say what the government's attitude was to you, what you achieved and why you are joining the Medical Women's Federation.

Further projects

1 Go to you local supermarket or food shop. Look for the herbs and spices. If possible, buy a selection and stick them in a notebook with sticky tape. Then look them up in a Herbal (like Culpepers) and explain what their healing qualities are.

2 Interview your parents, grandparents etc. Ask them about the healthcare they received when they were young. Think out the questions you want to ask them first. Write up your findings.

3 Collect newspaper items on hospitals and health. What issues are being reported? Do different newspapers cover the issues differently? What part do women and men play in these reports?

4 Look through some old magazines. Cut out advertisements for medicines, ointments etc. What do they tell you about medicine today? How are patent medicines different in the 20th century, compared with last century?

5 Interview men and women about their experiences of ill-health. Are there any differences or similarities? Think up your questions carefully beforehand. If possible record the interview on a tape recorder.

Further reading

There are very few accessible books about women in medicine.

M. V. Lyons, *Medicine in the Middle Ages*, Macmillan, 1984 (Has one chapter on women)

Mary Chamberlain, *Old Wives' Tales*, Virago, 1981 (A general overview)

Kate Campbell, *A History of Women in Medicine*, Hodder Press, 1938 (A general overview; a hard read)

Chapter 1

R. L. Verma and N. H. Keswani, *The Role of Women in Greco-Roman Medicine*, Studies in the History of Medicine, 1977

Chapter 2

Muriel Joy Hughes, *Women Healers in Medieval Life and Literature*, King's Crown Press, New York, 1943
Eileen Power, *Some Practitioners of Medicine in the Middle Ages*, Proceedings of the Royal Society of Medicine, 1923
The Paston Letters, ed. N. Davis, Oxford, 1958
Trotula, *Diseases of Women*, ed. Elizabeth Mason-Hohl, Ward Ritchie Press, 1940

Chapter 3

Leonard Guthrie, *Lady Sedley's Receipt Book, 1686, and other 17th Century Receipt Books*, Proceedings of the Royal Society of Medicine, 1913
John Blake, *The Compleat Housewife*, Bulletin of the History of Medicine, vol. 49, 1975.
Hannah Wolley, *The Accomplisht Ladys Delight*, 1675
William Buchon, *Domestic Medicine or the Family Physician*, 2nd edn London, 1772

Chapter 4

Christina Larner, *Enemies of God*, Basil Blackwell, 1981
K. Thomas, *Religion and the Decline of Magic*, Penguin, 1973
Barbara Ehrenreich and Diedre English, *Witches, Midwives and Nurses*, Readers' Publishing Co-operative, 1976

Chapter 5

Disbursements for the Parish of Lee, 18th Century, Manor House Local History Library
Alice Clark, *The Working Life of Women in the 17th Century*, Routledge and Sons, 1919
Elizabeth Blackwell, *A Curious Herbal: Containing Five Hundred Cuts of the most Useful in the Practice of Physik*, 1756

Chapter 6

Jean Donnison, *Midwives and Medical Men*, Heinemann, 1977
Audrey Eccles, *Obstetrics and Gynaecology in Tudor and Stuart England*, Croom Helm, 1982
Jean Towler and Joan Bramall, *Midwives in History and Society*, Croom Helm, 1986

Chapter 7

Letters of the Right Honourable Lady Mary Wortley Montagu, London, 1735

Genevieve Miller, *The Adoption of Inoculation for Smallpox in England and France*, University of Pennsylvania Press

Chapter 8

Neil Tonge and Michael Quincey, *Cholera and Public Health*, Macmillan, 1985
John Simon, *Public Health Report*, London, 1887
F. B. Smith, *The People's Health 1830–1910*, Croom Helm, 1979
Ladies' Sanitary Association Publications: *The Worth of Fresh Air*; *The Use of Pure Water*; *The Value of Good Food*, Fawcett Library, London
The English Woman's Journal, 1859 and 1860
Metropolitan Borough of St Marylebone *Report of the Medical Officer of Health*, 1908, GLC Record Office, London

Chapter 9

Derek Fraser, *The New Poor Law in the 19th Century*, Macmillan, 1976
Irvine London, *Medical Care and the General Practitioner, 1750–1850*, OUP, 1987
Minute Books of Lambeth Workhouse, 1836, 1842, GLC Record Office, London
Elizabeth Roberts, *A Woman's Place*, 1984

Chapter 10

The English Woman's Journal, 1856, 1860, 1861
Sophia Jex Blake, *Medical Women*, Oliphant, Edinburgh, 1886
Victorian Women: A Documentary Account of Women's Lives in 19th Century England, France and the United States, ed. Erna Olafson Hellerstein, Leslie Parker Home and Karen M. Offen, Harvester Press, 1981
Patricia Hollis, *Women in Public*, George Allen and Unwin, 1979
The Wonderful Adventures of Mrs Seacole in Many Lands, ed. Z. Alexander and A. Dewjee, Falling Wall Press, 1984

Chapter 11

Diaries and *Papers* in the Imperial War Museum

Chapter 12

Health and Personal Services Statistics for England, DHSS, April 1987

Glossary

act *see* bill

bill a proposal for reform presented to Parliament. If it is agreed upon by the House of Commons and the House of Lords then it becomes an act, and then law

bleeding (leeching) a form of medical treatment which involved taking blood from a patient. It was often done by putting leeches on a vein in the patient's arm and the leeches then sucked the blood

choleric one of the four humours. Yellow bile. Too much of this would make a person angry and irritable

consultant a doctor or surgeon who holds the highest position in a particular branch of medicine at a hospital

embalming preserving a dead body. This technique was developed by the Ancient Egyptians. The internal organs were removed and stored in special jars. The body was then treated with chemicals, and mummified

excommunicated thrown out of the Church

gangrene decaying tissue

Inquisition a special court set up in the late Middle Ages to get rid of heretics – people who did not accept the ideas of the Roman Catholic Church

melancholic one of the four humours. Black bile. A person who is melancholic has a tendency to be sad, gloomy and depressed

phlegmatic one of the four humours. Phlegm. A person who is phlegmatic is sluggish, apathetic, and not easily excited

physician a doctor who has a university degree

physiology the study of how living things work

puerperal fever a serious illness, formerly widespread, contracted by women in childbirth. The womb becomes infected, causing a high fever from which the woman generally died

rate book record kept by each parish with the amount of rates (money) collected from each householder and an account of how the money was spent

rolls (parliamentary) an official record of what happened in Parliament. The record was written on long pieces of parchment which were then rolled up

sanguine one of the four humours. Blood. A person who is sanguine has a red complexion, is bold, cheerful and amorous

sepsis pus and matter from an infected wound

surgeon doctor who deals with internal illnesses and performs operations. In the Middle Ages they were linked with barbers. They broke this link in Britain in 1745 when the Royal Company of Surgeons was founded

VAD Women's Voluntary Aid Detachment